SUBTRACTION 0-12

Workbook Math Essentials

Children's Arithmetic Books

PROFESSOR GUSTO
EDUCATIONAL & INFORMATIVE BOOKS FOR CHILDREN
(PRE-K / K-12)

Subtraction Exercises

Exercise No. 1

1.)
$$\begin{array}{r} 4 \\ -\ \ 0 \\ \hline \end{array}$$

2.)
$$\begin{array}{r} 11 \\ -\ 10 \\ \hline \end{array}$$

3.)
$$\begin{array}{r} 12 \\ -\ \ 8 \\ \hline \end{array}$$

4.)

5.)

6.)

7.)
$$\begin{array}{r} 9 \\ -\ \ 3 \\ \hline \end{array}$$

8.)
$$\begin{array}{r} 8 \\ -\ \ 7 \\ \hline \end{array}$$

9.)
$$\begin{array}{r} 12 \\ -\ \ 1 \\ \hline \end{array}$$

Exercise No. 2

1.) $10 - 7 =$ ____

2.) $12 - 7 =$ ____

3.) $4 - 4 =$ ____

4.) $11 - 8 =$ ____

5.) $5 - 2 =$ ____

6.) $11 - 6 =$ ____

7.) $6 - 6 =$ ____

8.) $1 - 0 =$ ____

9.) $1 - 0 =$ ____

Exercise No. 3

1.) $\begin{array}{r} 6 \\ -\ 1 \\ \hline \end{array}$

2.) $\begin{array}{r} 8 \\ -\ 7 \\ \hline \end{array}$

3.) $\begin{array}{r} 5 \\ -\ 1 \\ \hline \end{array}$

4.) $\begin{array}{r} 5 \\ -\ 2 \\ \hline \end{array}$

5.) $\begin{array}{r} 6 \\ -\ 2 \\ \hline \end{array}$

6.) $\begin{array}{r} 5 \\ -\ 2 \\ \hline \end{array}$

7.) $\begin{array}{r} 11 \\ -\ 3 \\ \hline \end{array}$

8.) $\begin{array}{r} 7 \\ -\ 3 \\ \hline \end{array}$

9.) $\begin{array}{r} 11 \\ -\ 6 \\ \hline \end{array}$

Exercise No. 4

1.) $$\begin{array}{r} 12 \\ -\ \ 9 \\ \hline \end{array}$$

2.) $$\begin{array}{r} 4 \\ -\ \ 3 \\ \hline \end{array}$$

3.) $$\begin{array}{r} 10 \\ -\ \ 7 \\ \hline \end{array}$$

4.) $$\begin{array}{r} 12 \\ -\ \ 0 \\ \hline \end{array}$$

5.) $$\begin{array}{r} 3 \\ -\ \ 1 \\ \hline \end{array}$$

6.) $$\begin{array}{r} 10 \\ -\ \ 6 \\ \hline \end{array}$$

7.) $$\begin{array}{r} 1 \\ -\ \ 0 \\ \hline \end{array}$$

8.) $$\begin{array}{r} 9 \\ -\ \ 7 \\ \hline \end{array}$$

9.) $$\begin{array}{r} 8 \\ -\ \ 0 \\ \hline \end{array}$$

Exercise No. 5

1.) $$\begin{array}{r} 7 \\ -\ \ 4 \\ \hline \end{array}$$

2.) $$\begin{array}{r} 10 \\ -\ \ 6 \\ \hline \end{array}$$

3.) $$\begin{array}{r} 11 \\ -\ \ 1 \\ \hline \end{array}$$

4.) $$\begin{array}{r} 7 \\ -\ \ 2 \\ \hline \end{array}$$

5.) $$\begin{array}{r} 10 \\ -\ \ 9 \\ \hline \end{array}$$

6.) $$\begin{array}{r} 3 \\ -\ \ 0 \\ \hline \end{array}$$

7.) $$\begin{array}{r} 6 \\ -\ \ 5 \\ \hline \end{array}$$

8.) $$\begin{array}{r} 6 \\ -\ \ 6 \\ \hline \end{array}$$

9.) $$\begin{array}{r} 3 \\ -\ \ 0 \\ \hline \end{array}$$

Exercise No. 6

1.) $\begin{array}{r} 10 \\ -\ \ 9 \\ \hline \end{array}$

2.) $\begin{array}{r} 2 \\ -\ \ 2 \\ \hline \end{array}$

3.) $\begin{array}{r} 11 \\ -\ \ 8 \\ \hline \end{array}$

4.) $\begin{array}{r} 9 \\ -\ \ 2 \\ \hline \end{array}$

5.) $\begin{array}{r} 8 \\ -\ \ 5 \\ \hline \end{array}$

6.) $\begin{array}{r} 1 \\ -\ \ 0 \\ \hline \end{array}$

7.) $\begin{array}{r} 7 \\ -\ \ 4 \\ \hline \end{array}$

8.) $\begin{array}{r} 8 \\ -\ \ 0 \\ \hline \end{array}$

9.) $\begin{array}{r} 12 \\ -\ \ 8 \\ \hline \end{array}$

Exercise No. 7

1.) $\begin{array}{r} 8 \\ -\ 1 \\ \hline \end{array}$

2.) $\begin{array}{r} 12 \\ -\ 0 \\ \hline \end{array}$

3.) $\begin{array}{r} 10 \\ -\ 1 \\ \hline \end{array}$

4.) $\begin{array}{r} 12 \\ -\ 3 \\ \hline \end{array}$

5.) $\begin{array}{r} 3 \\ -\ 2 \\ \hline \end{array}$

6.) $\begin{array}{r} 7 \\ -\ 6 \\ \hline \end{array}$

7.) $\begin{array}{r} 10 \\ -\ 7 \\ \hline \end{array}$

8.) $\begin{array}{r} 2 \\ -\ 0 \\ \hline \end{array}$

9.) $\begin{array}{r} 8 \\ -\ 3 \\ \hline \end{array}$

Exercise No. 8

1.) $\begin{array}{r} 9 \\ -\ 6 \\ \hline \end{array}$

2.) $\begin{array}{r} 11 \\ -\ 7 \\ \hline \end{array}$

3.) $\begin{array}{r} 9 \\ -\ 8 \\ \hline \end{array}$

4.) $\begin{array}{r} 9 \\ -\ 3 \\ \hline \end{array}$

5.) $\begin{array}{r} 5 \\ -\ 1 \\ \hline \end{array}$

6.) $\begin{array}{r} 3 \\ -\ 1 \\ \hline \end{array}$

7.) $\begin{array}{r} 6 \\ -\ 2 \\ \hline \end{array}$

8.) $\begin{array}{r} 9 \\ -\ 0 \\ \hline \end{array}$

9.) $\begin{array}{r} 11 \\ -\ 5 \\ \hline \end{array}$

Exercise No. 9

1.) $\begin{array}{r} 12 \\ -\ \ 8 \\ \hline \end{array}$

2.) $\begin{array}{r} 10 \\ -\ \ 4 \\ \hline \end{array}$

3.) $\begin{array}{r} 4 \\ -\ \ 0 \\ \hline \end{array}$

4.) $\begin{array}{r} 9 \\ -\ \ 6 \\ \hline \end{array}$

5.) $\begin{array}{r} 9 \\ -\ \ 8 \\ \hline \end{array}$

6.) $\begin{array}{r} 4 \\ -\ \ 2 \\ \hline \end{array}$

7.) $\begin{array}{r} 11 \\ -\ \ 3 \\ \hline \end{array}$

8.) $\begin{array}{r} 8 \\ -\ \ 2 \\ \hline \end{array}$

9.) $\begin{array}{r} 2 \\ -\ \ 2 \\ \hline \end{array}$

Exercise No. 10

1.) $\begin{array}{r} 11 \\ -\ \ 8 \\ \hline \end{array}$

2.) $\begin{array}{r} 12 \\ -\ \ 0 \\ \hline \end{array}$

3.) $\begin{array}{r} 11 \\ -\ \ 5 \\ \hline \end{array}$

4.) $\begin{array}{r} 3 \\ -\ \ 2 \\ \hline \end{array}$

5.) $\begin{array}{r} 11 \\ -\ \ 7 \\ \hline \end{array}$

6.) $\begin{array}{r} 9 \\ -\ \ 6 \\ \hline \end{array}$

7.) $\begin{array}{r} 10 \\ -\ \ 8 \\ \hline \end{array}$

8.) $\begin{array}{r} 7 \\ -\ \ 6 \\ \hline \end{array}$

9.) $\begin{array}{r} 10 \\ -\ \ 1 \\ \hline \end{array}$

Exercise No. 1

1.) $9 - 4 =$ ____

2.) $9 - 0 =$ ____

3.) $3 - 2 =$ ____

4.) $1 - 1 =$ ____

5.) $12 - 11 =$ ____

6.) $12 - 1 =$ ____

7.) $8 - 0 =$ ____

8.) $7 - 4 =$ ____

9.) $6 - 2 =$ ____

Exercise No. 12

1.)
```
   6
-  4
____
```

4.)
```
  11
-  0
____
```

7.)
```
   6
-  1
____
```

2.)
```
  12
-  1
____
```

5.)
```
   5
-  0
____
```

8.)
```
   3
-  2
____
```

3.)
```
   5
-  5
____
```

6.)
```
  11
-  6
____
```

9.)
```
   6
-  4
____
```

Exercise No. 13

1.) $$\begin{array}{r} 6 \\ -\quad 1 \\ \hline \end{array}$$

2.) $$\begin{array}{r} 11 \\ -\quad 3 \\ \hline \end{array}$$

3.) $$\begin{array}{r} 8 \\ -\quad 7 \\ \hline \end{array}$$

4.) $$\begin{array}{r} 11 \\ -\quad 7 \\ \hline \end{array}$$

5.) $$\begin{array}{r} 8 \\ -\quad 0 \\ \hline \end{array}$$

6.) $$\begin{array}{r} 8 \\ -\quad 1 \\ \hline \end{array}$$

7.) $$\begin{array}{r} 12 \\ -\quad 3 \\ \hline \end{array}$$

8.) $$\begin{array}{r} 6 \\ -\quad 4 \\ \hline \end{array}$$

9.) $$\begin{array}{r} 7 \\ -\quad 2 \\ \hline \end{array}$$

Exercise No. 14

1.)
$$\begin{array}{r} 10 \\ -\ \ 5 \\ \hline \end{array}$$

4.)
$$\begin{array}{r} 2 \\ -\ \ 0 \\ \hline \end{array}$$

7.)
$$\begin{array}{r} 11 \\ -\ \ 7 \\ \hline \end{array}$$

2.)
$$\begin{array}{r} 10 \\ -\ \ 9 \\ \hline \end{array}$$

5.)
$$\begin{array}{r} 5 \\ -\ \ 0 \\ \hline \end{array}$$

8.)
$$\begin{array}{r} 6 \\ -\ \ 0 \\ \hline \end{array}$$

3.)
$$\begin{array}{r} 7 \\ -\ \ 2 \\ \hline \end{array}$$

6.)
$$\begin{array}{r} 10 \\ -\ \ 1 \\ \hline \end{array}$$

9.)
$$\begin{array}{r} 12 \\ -\ 10 \\ \hline \end{array}$$

Exercise No. 15

1.) $\begin{array}{r} 11 \\ -\quad 4 \\ \hline \end{array}$

2.) $\begin{array}{r} 12 \\ -\quad 7 \\ \hline \end{array}$

3.) $\begin{array}{r} 8 \\ -\quad 0 \\ \hline \end{array}$

4.) $\begin{array}{r} 2 \\ -\quad 0 \\ \hline \end{array}$

5.) $\begin{array}{r} 10 \\ -\quad 7 \\ \hline \end{array}$

6.) $\begin{array}{r} 10 \\ -\quad 7 \\ \hline \end{array}$

7.) $\begin{array}{r} 6 \\ -\quad 1 \\ \hline \end{array}$

8.) $\begin{array}{r} 8 \\ -\quad 5 \\ \hline \end{array}$

9.) $\begin{array}{r} 6 \\ -\quad 3 \\ \hline \end{array}$

Exercise No. 16

1.) $$\begin{array}{r} 12 \\ -\ \ 1 \\ \hline \end{array}$$

2.) $$\begin{array}{r} 12 \\ -\ \ 3 \\ \hline \end{array}$$

3.) $$\begin{array}{r} 10 \\ -\ \ 7 \\ \hline \end{array}$$

4.) $$\begin{array}{r} 11 \\ -\ \ 2 \\ \hline \end{array}$$

5.) $$\begin{array}{r} 6 \\ -\ \ 3 \\ \hline \end{array}$$

6.) $$\begin{array}{r} 10 \\ -\ \ 1 \\ \hline \end{array}$$

7.) $$\begin{array}{r} 9 \\ -\ \ 6 \\ \hline \end{array}$$

8.) $$\begin{array}{r} 7 \\ -\ \ 4 \\ \hline \end{array}$$

9.) $$\begin{array}{r} 9 \\ -\ \ 4 \\ \hline \end{array}$$

Exercise No. 17

1.) $\begin{array}{r} 9 \\ -\ \ 6 \\ \hline \end{array}$

2.) $\begin{array}{r} 4 \\ -\ \ 2 \\ \hline \end{array}$

3.) $\begin{array}{r} 7 \\ -\ \ 6 \\ \hline \end{array}$

4.) $\begin{array}{r} 5 \\ -\ \ 3 \\ \hline \end{array}$

5.) $\begin{array}{r} 12 \\ -\ \ 4 \\ \hline \end{array}$

6.) $\begin{array}{r} 7 \\ -\ \ 0 \\ \hline \end{array}$

7.) $\begin{array}{r} 7 \\ -\ \ 6 \\ \hline \end{array}$

8.) $\begin{array}{r} 7 \\ -\ \ 0 \\ \hline \end{array}$

9.) $\begin{array}{r} 12 \\ -\ \ 5 \\ \hline \end{array}$

Exercise No. 18

1.) $\begin{array}{r} 8 \\ -\ 5 \\ \hline \end{array}$

2.) $\begin{array}{r} 0 \\ -\ 0 \\ \hline \end{array}$

3.) $\begin{array}{r} 11 \\ -\ 6 \\ \hline \end{array}$

4.) $\begin{array}{r} 11 \\ -\ 5 \\ \hline \end{array}$

5.) $\begin{array}{r} 10 \\ -\ 1 \\ \hline \end{array}$

6.) $\begin{array}{r} 8 \\ -\ 3 \\ \hline \end{array}$

7.) $\begin{array}{r} 10 \\ -\ 4 \\ \hline \end{array}$

8.) $\begin{array}{r} 5 \\ -\ 2 \\ \hline \end{array}$

9.) $\begin{array}{r} 12 \\ -\ 8 \\ \hline \end{array}$

Exercise No. 19

1.) $\begin{array}{r} 4 \\ -\ \ 0 \\ \hline \end{array}$

2.) $\begin{array}{r} 12 \\ -\ 10 \\ \hline \end{array}$

3.) $\begin{array}{r} 9 \\ -\ \ 4 \\ \hline \end{array}$

4.) $\begin{array}{r} 7 \\ -\ \ 5 \\ \hline \end{array}$

5.) $\begin{array}{r} 9 \\ -\ \ 1 \\ \hline \end{array}$

6.) $\begin{array}{r} 8 \\ -\ \ 7 \\ \hline \end{array}$

7.) $\begin{array}{r} 3 \\ -\ \ 0 \\ \hline \end{array}$

8.) $\begin{array}{r} 4 \\ -\ \ 0 \\ \hline \end{array}$

9.) $\begin{array}{r} 11 \\ -\ 11 \\ \hline \end{array}$

Exercise No. 20

1.) $4 - 4 =$ ____

2.) $10 - 3 =$ ____

3.) $11 - 5 =$ ____

4.) $5 - 2 =$ ____

5.) $2 - 0 =$ ____

6.) $10 - 8 =$ ____

7.) $12 - 8 =$ ____

8.) $9 - 7 =$ ____

9.) $2 - 0 =$ ____

Exercise No. 21

1.) 12 − 5 = ____

2.) 10 − 1 = ____

3.) 7 − 0 = ____

4.) 6 − 5 = ____

5.) 12 − 11 = ____

6.) 10 − 6 = ____

7.) 7 − 3 = ____

8.) 8 − 8 = ____

9.) 3 − 3 = ____

Exercise No. 22

1.) $\begin{array}{r} 11 \\ -\ 10 \\ \hline \end{array}$

2.) $\begin{array}{r} 7 \\ -\ 0 \\ \hline \end{array}$

3.) $\begin{array}{r} 5 \\ -\ 5 \\ \hline \end{array}$

4.) $\begin{array}{r} 10 \\ -\ 4 \\ \hline \end{array}$

5.) $\begin{array}{r} 9 \\ -\ 4 \\ \hline \end{array}$

6.) $\begin{array}{r} 9 \\ -\ 6 \\ \hline \end{array}$

7.) $\begin{array}{r} 11 \\ -\ 1 \\ \hline \end{array}$

8.) $\begin{array}{r} 6 \\ -\ 4 \\ \hline \end{array}$

9.) $\begin{array}{r} 7 \\ -\ 3 \\ \hline \end{array}$

Exercise No. 23

1.) $$\begin{array}{r} 3 \\ -\ \ 1 \\ \hline \end{array}$$

2.) $$\begin{array}{r} 9 \\ -\ \ 0 \\ \hline \end{array}$$

3.) $$\begin{array}{r} 12 \\ -\ 11 \\ \hline \end{array}$$

4.) $$\begin{array}{r} 10 \\ -\ \ 5 \\ \hline \end{array}$$

5.) $$\begin{array}{r} 9 \\ -\ \ 5 \\ \hline \end{array}$$

6.) $$\begin{array}{r} 6 \\ -\ \ 6 \\ \hline \end{array}$$

7.) $$\begin{array}{r} 12 \\ -\ \ 2 \\ \hline \end{array}$$

8.) $$\begin{array}{r} 8 \\ -\ \ 3 \\ \hline \end{array}$$

9.) $$\begin{array}{r} 7 \\ -\ \ 0 \\ \hline \end{array}$$

Exercise No. 24

1.) $\begin{array}{r} 9 \\ -\ 0 \\ \hline \end{array}$

2.) $\begin{array}{r} 11 \\ -\ 4 \\ \hline \end{array}$

3.) $\begin{array}{r} 10 \\ -\ 1 \\ \hline \end{array}$

4.) $\begin{array}{r} 12 \\ -\ 10 \\ \hline \end{array}$

5.) $\begin{array}{r} 9 \\ -\ 0 \\ \hline \end{array}$

6.) $\begin{array}{r} 8 \\ -\ 6 \\ \hline \end{array}$

7.) $\begin{array}{r} 7 \\ -\ 4 \\ \hline \end{array}$

8.) $\begin{array}{r} 5 \\ -\ 4 \\ \hline \end{array}$

9.) $\begin{array}{r} 5 \\ -\ 2 \\ \hline \end{array}$

Exercise No. 25

1.) $\begin{array}{r} 8 \\ -\ \ 0 \\ \hline \end{array}$

2.) $\begin{array}{r} 9 \\ -\ \ 3 \\ \hline \end{array}$

3.) $\begin{array}{r} 2 \\ -\ \ 0 \\ \hline \end{array}$

4.) $\begin{array}{r} 12 \\ -\ 11 \\ \hline \end{array}$

5.) $\begin{array}{r} 10 \\ -\ 10 \\ \hline \end{array}$

6.) $\begin{array}{r} 9 \\ -\ \ 3 \\ \hline \end{array}$

7.) $\begin{array}{r} 6 \\ -\ \ 4 \\ \hline \end{array}$

8.) $\begin{array}{r} 7 \\ -\ \ 7 \\ \hline \end{array}$

9.) $\begin{array}{r} 11 \\ -\ \ 4 \\ \hline \end{array}$

Exercise No. 26

1.) $\begin{array}{r} 10 \\ -\ \ 2 \\ \hline \end{array}$

2.) $\begin{array}{r} 1 \\ -\ \ 0 \\ \hline \end{array}$

3.) $\begin{array}{r} 12 \\ -\ \ 6 \\ \hline \end{array}$

4.) $\begin{array}{r} 2 \\ -\ \ 1 \\ \hline \end{array}$

5.) $\begin{array}{r} 11 \\ -\ 10 \\ \hline \end{array}$

6.) $\begin{array}{r} 6 \\ -\ \ 3 \\ \hline \end{array}$

7.) $\begin{array}{r} 8 \\ -\ \ 1 \\ \hline \end{array}$

8.) $\begin{array}{r} 8 \\ -\ \ 4 \\ \hline \end{array}$

9.) $\begin{array}{r} 9 \\ -\ \ 9 \\ \hline \end{array}$

Exercise No. 27

1.) $\begin{array}{r} 11 \\ -\ \ 5 \\ \hline \end{array}$

2.) $\begin{array}{r} 7 \\ -\ \ 3 \\ \hline \end{array}$

3.) $\begin{array}{r} 1 \\ -\ \ 1 \\ \hline \end{array}$

4.) $\begin{array}{r} 10 \\ -\ \ 4 \\ \hline \end{array}$

5.) $\begin{array}{r} 10 \\ -\ \ 0 \\ \hline \end{array}$

6.) $\begin{array}{r} 5 \\ -\ \ 5 \\ \hline \end{array}$

7.) $\begin{array}{r} 8 \\ -\ \ 4 \\ \hline \end{array}$

8.) $\begin{array}{r} 9 \\ -\ \ 8 \\ \hline \end{array}$

9.) $\begin{array}{r} 10 \\ -\ \ 9 \\ \hline \end{array}$

Exercise No. 28

1.) $\begin{array}{r} 6 \\ -\ 0 \\ \hline \end{array}$

2.) $\begin{array}{r} 12 \\ -\ 4 \\ \hline \end{array}$

3.) $\begin{array}{r} 12 \\ -\ 0 \\ \hline \end{array}$

4.) $\begin{array}{r} 6 \\ -\ 3 \\ \hline \end{array}$

5.) $\begin{array}{r} 7 \\ -\ 6 \\ \hline \end{array}$

6.) $\begin{array}{r} 8 \\ -\ 6 \\ \hline \end{array}$

7.) $\begin{array}{r} 3 \\ -\ 3 \\ \hline \end{array}$

8.) $\begin{array}{r} 7 \\ -\ 1 \\ \hline \end{array}$

9.) $\begin{array}{r} 10 \\ -\ 2 \\ \hline \end{array}$

Exercise No. 29

1.) $\begin{array}{r} 9 \\ -\ \ 5 \\ \hline \end{array}$

2.) $\begin{array}{r} 7 \\ -\ \ 1 \\ \hline \end{array}$

3.) $\begin{array}{r} 11 \\ -\ \ 4 \\ \hline \end{array}$

4.) $\begin{array}{r} 6 \\ -\ \ 4 \\ \hline \end{array}$

5.) $\begin{array}{r} 9 \\ -\ \ 5 \\ \hline \end{array}$

6.) $\begin{array}{r} 6 \\ -\ \ 3 \\ \hline \end{array}$

7.) $\begin{array}{r} 6 \\ -\ \ 1 \\ \hline \end{array}$

8.) $\begin{array}{r} 9 \\ -\ \ 0 \\ \hline \end{array}$

9.) $\begin{array}{r} 11 \\ -\ \ 1 \\ \hline \end{array}$

Exercise No. 30

1.) $\begin{array}{r} 8 \\ -\ 8 \\ \hline \end{array}$

2.) $\begin{array}{r} 12 \\ -\ 2 \\ \hline \end{array}$

3.) $\begin{array}{r} 3 \\ -\ 3 \\ \hline \end{array}$

4.) $\begin{array}{r} 12 \\ -\ 1 \\ \hline \end{array}$

5.) $\begin{array}{r} 9 \\ -\ 5 \\ \hline \end{array}$

6.) $\begin{array}{r} 6 \\ -\ 0 \\ \hline \end{array}$

7.) $\begin{array}{r} 5 \\ -\ 3 \\ \hline \end{array}$

8.) $\begin{array}{r} 8 \\ -\ 7 \\ \hline \end{array}$

9.) $\begin{array}{r} 10 \\ -\ 0 \\ \hline \end{array}$

Exercise No. 31

1.) $\begin{array}{r} 12 \\ -\quad 7 \\ \hline \end{array}$

2.) $\begin{array}{r} 8 \\ -\quad 0 \\ \hline \end{array}$

3.) $\begin{array}{r} 10 \\ -\quad 4 \\ \hline \end{array}$

4.) $\begin{array}{r} 11 \\ -\quad 3 \\ \hline \end{array}$

5.) $\begin{array}{r} 11 \\ -\quad 9 \\ \hline \end{array}$

6.) $\begin{array}{r} 10 \\ -\quad 6 \\ \hline \end{array}$

7.) $\begin{array}{r} 8 \\ -\quad 5 \\ \hline \end{array}$

8.) $\begin{array}{r} 1 \\ -\quad 0 \\ \hline \end{array}$

9.) $\begin{array}{r} 4 \\ -\quad 3 \\ \hline \end{array}$

Exercise No. 32

1.) $\begin{array}{r} 2 \\ -\quad 2 \\ \hline \end{array}$

2.) $\begin{array}{r} 3 \\ -\quad 0 \\ \hline \end{array}$

3.) $\begin{array}{r} 7 \\ -\quad 1 \\ \hline \end{array}$

4.) $\begin{array}{r} 9 \\ -\quad 1 \\ \hline \end{array}$

5.) $\begin{array}{r} 8 \\ -\quad 8 \\ \hline \end{array}$

6.) $\begin{array}{r} 7 \\ -\quad 2 \\ \hline \end{array}$

7.) $\begin{array}{r} 4 \\ -\quad 2 \\ \hline \end{array}$

8.) $\begin{array}{r} 12 \\ -\quad 6 \\ \hline \end{array}$

9.) $\begin{array}{r} 6 \\ -\quad 2 \\ \hline \end{array}$

ANSWERS

Exercise No. 1.

1.) 5
2.) 1
3.) 4
4.) 3
5.) 4
6.) 3
7.) 8
8.) 4
9.) 5

Exercise No. 2.

1.) 3
2.) 1
3.) 3
4.) 12
5.) 2
6.) 4
7.) 1
8.) 2
9.) 8

Exercise No. 3.

1.) 3
2.) 4
3.) 10
4.) 2
5.) 11
6.) 1
7.) 3
8.) 6
9.) 5

Exercise No. 4.

1.) 3
2.) 7
3.) 8
4.) 1
5.) 11
6.) 7
7.) 1
8.) 5
9.) 3

Exercise No. 5.

1.) 5
2.) 8
3.) 9
4.) 5
5.) 1
6.) 3
7.) 1
8.) 0
9.) 3

Exercise No. 6.

1.) 1
2.) 0
3.) 3
4.) 7
5.) 3
6.) 1
7.) 3
8.) 8
9.) 4

Exercise No. 7.

1.) 7
2.) 12
3.) 9
4.) 9
5.) 1
6.) 1
7.) 3
8.) 2
9.) 5

Exercise No. 8.

1.) 3
2.) 4
3.) 1
4.) 6
5.) 4
6.) 2
7.) 4
8.) 9
9.) 6

Exercise No. 9.

1.) 4
2.) 6
3.) 4
4.) 3
5.) 1
6.) 2
7.) 8
8.) 6
9.) 0

Exercise No. 10.

1.) 3
2.) 12
3.) 6
4.) 1
5.) 4
6.) 3
7.) 2
8.) 1
9.) 9

Exercise No. 11.

1.) 5
2.) 9
3.) 1
4.) 0
5.) 1
6.) 11
7.) 8
8.) 3
9.) 4

Exercise No. 12.

1.) 2
2.) 11
3.) 0
4.) 11
5.) 5
6.) 5
7.) 5
8.) 1
9.) 2

Exercise No. 13.

1.) 5
2.) 8
3.) 1
4.) 4
5.) 8
6.) 7
7.) 9
8.) 2
9.) 5

Exercise No. 14.

1.) 5
2.) 9
3.) 5
4.) 2
5.) 5
6.) 9
7.) 4
8.) 6
9.) 2

Exercise No. 15.

1.) 7
2.) 5
3.) 8
4.) 2
5.) 3
6.) 3
7.) 5
8.) 3
9.) 3

Exercise No. 16.

1.) 11
2.) 9
3.) 3
4.) 9
5.) 3
6.) 9
7.) 3
8.) 3
9.) 5

Exercise No. 17.

1.) 3
2.) 2
3.) 1
4.) 2
5.) 8
6.) 7
7.) 1
8.) 7
9.) 7

Exercise No. 18.

1.) 3
2.) 0
3.) 5
4.) 6
5.) 9
6.) 5
7.) 6
8.) 3
9.) 4

Exercise No. 19.

1.) 4
2.) 2
3.) 5
4.) 2
5.) 8
6.) 1
7.) 3
8.) 4
9.) 0

Exercise No. 20.

1.) 0
2.) 7
3.) 6
4.) 3
5.) 2
6.) 2
7.) 4
8.) 2
9.) 2

Exercise No. 21.

1.) 7
2.) 9
3.) 7
4.) 1
5.) 1
6.) 4
7.) 4
8.) 0
9.) 0

Exercise No. 22.

1.) 1
2.) 7
3.) 0
4.) 6
5.) 5
6.) 3
7.) 10
8.) 2
9.) 4

Exercise No. 23.

1.) 2
2.) 9
3.) 1
4.) 5
5.) 4
6.) 0
7.) 10
8.) 5
9.) 7

Exercise No. 24.

1.) 9
2.) 7
3.) 9
4.) 2
5.) 9
6.) 2
7.) 3
8.) 1
9.) 3

Exercise No. 25.

1.) 8
2.) 6
3.) 2
4.) 1
5.) 0
6.) 6
7.) 2
8.) 0
9.) 7

Exercise No. 26.

1.) 8
2.) 1
3.) 6
4.) 1
5.) 1
6.) 3
7.) 7
8.) 4
9.) 0

Exercise No. 27.

1.) 6
2.) 4
3.) 0
4.) 6
5.) 10
6.) 0
7.) 4
8.) 1
9.) 1

Exercise No. 28.

1.) 6
2.) 8
3.) 12
4.) 3
5.) 1
6.) 2
7.) 0
8.) 6
9.) 8

Exercise No. 29.

1.) 4
2.) 6
3.) 7
4.) 2
5.) 4
6.) 3
7.) 5
8.) 9
9.) 10

Exercise No. 30.

1.) 0
2.) 10
3.) 0
4.) 11
5.) 4
6.) 6
7.) 2
8.) 1
9.) 10

Exercise No. 31.

1.) 5
2.) 8
3.) 6
4.) 8
5.) 2
6.) 4
7.) 3
8.) 1
9.) 1

Exercise No. 32.

1.) 0
2.) 3
3.) 6
4.) 8
5.) 0
6.) 5
7.) 2
8.) 6
9.) 4

www.ingramcontent.com/pod-product-compliance
Lightning Source LLC
LaVergne TN
LVHW082254070426
835507LV00037B/2291
* 9 7 8 1 6 8 3 2 1 3 2 6 0 *